World War II
Pacific Theater
PUZZLE BOOK

GRAB A PENCIL PRESS

CARLISLE, MASSACHUSETTS

World War II Pacific Theater Puzzle Book

Copyright © 2016 Applewood Books, Inc.

All rights reserved. No part of this book may be reproduced in any form or by any electronic or mechanical means without permission in writing from the publisher, except by a reviewer who may quote brief passages in a review.

ISBN: 978-0-9882885-7-7

Published by
GRAB A PENCIL PRESS
an imprint of Applewood Books
Carlisle, Massachusetts 01741
www.grabapencilpress.com

10 9 8 7 6 5 4 3 2 1

Manufactured in the United States of America

World War II
Pacific Theater
PUZZLE BOOK

"Among the men who fought on Iwo Jima, uncommon valor was a common virtue."

    Admiral Chester W. Nimitz
    March 16, 1945

U.S.S. YORKTOWN

The Japanese attack on Pearl Harbor December 7, 1941, triggered the official entry of the United States into World War II. Targets of the two-day Japanese attack included a large area of the Pacific Ocean region: Thailand; Malaya; Singapore; and U.S. military bases in Guam, Wake Island, and the Philippines. Unlike the war in Europe, fought on land, the Pacific war was a number of battles fought over islands and island chains covering a vast amount of ocean territory.

    Early on, Japan was victorious in battles in the southwest Pacific. The takeover of the Philippines forced a retreat by U.S. Army General Douglas MacArthur, who vowed, "I will return." It wasn't until the summer of 1942 that the United States went on the offense against Japan. The Allies, led by the United States, won the Battles of Coral Sea and Midway and turned the tide of war. After a hard-fought battle in 1943, Guadalcanal proved another decisive win for Allied forces. Many Japanese-held islands were retaken under the command of Admiral Chester Nimitz. During the summer of 1944 Saipan and Guam were won back from the Japanese. General MacArthur's promised return to the Philippines was marked by victories at the Battle of Leyte Gulf and at Luzon. In early 1945 the Chinese were also able to win back territory taken by Japan. The U.S. taking of Iwo Jima in March 1945, with the famous raising of the Stars and Stripes on Mount Suribachi, brought war to the doorstep of Japan's mainland. With Japan unwilling to give up a losing fight, President Truman ordered the dropping of atomic bombs on the Japanese cities of Hiroshima and Nagasaki in August of 1945. This devastating act killed approximately 100,000 Japanese citizens and brought the Pacific war to a quick close. V-J (Victory in Japan) Day was celebrated September 2, 1945, with Japan's surrender on the U.S.S. *Missouri*.

    This book highlights important battles fought in the Pacific Ocean, beginning with the Japanese attack on Pearl Harbor and ending with the atomic bombs dropped on Japan. General MacArthur and Admiral Nimitz were key military leaders in the Pacific Theater. Breaking the Japanese code was an important part of the Allied effort in the defeat of Japan. The war in the Pacific tested the might and fight of Allied forces and resulted in a victory in which "uncommon valor was a common virtue" indeed.

PUZZLE ANSWERS ON BACK PAGES

U.S.S. *ARIZONA* MEMORIAL IN PEARL HARBOR

Names & Places of WWII

```
O T O M A M A Y E C H A M A R P
A J I N E T E N T O N H R E O E
N E V I G E O K I N A W A T U A
G U K A P L U H A S N S B Y C R
U L S T A S H T M A E A A E I L
A O N G T A M I J O W I A L G H
D M A R E M S L H O R A M T H A
A Y A B O R I T A C S N A E A R
L F O M A S N D R H I O C S A B
C N R C Y E H O W E A Z A T D O
A N E H R A W R D A H I R A W R
N I M I T Z A B E K Y R T N I T
A R O D I G E R R O C A H L N E
L P H I L I P P I N E S U B K L
R E A M I H S O R I H S R A Y I
B H A N A D L O T E R U W O H N
```

Find the following:

PEARL HARBOR	MIDWAY	IWO JIMA	PHILIPPINES
OKINAWA	CORREGIDOR	YAMAMOTO	BATAAN
MACARTHUR	NIMITZ	ENOLA GAY	WAKE
GUADALCANAL	USS ARIZONA	HIROSHIMA	LEYTE

Pacific War Battles & Motherlands

Match the Pacific War battle site with the mother country or commonwealth of the territory or country.

1. Battle of New Guinea
2. Battle of Iwo Jima
3. Battle of Corregidor
4. Battle of Prachuap Khiri Khan
5. Battle of Guadalcanal
6. Battle of Timor
7. Battle of Guam
8. Battle of Noemfoor
9. Battle of West Hunan

___ a. China
___ b. Philippines
___ c. Netherlands
___ d. Japan
___ e. Australia
___ f. United Kingdom
___ g. Thailand
___ h. Portugal
___ i. United States

AIRCRAFT ATTACK BRITISH BATTLESHIP, BY TERENCE CUNEO

U.S. NAVY SOLDIERS RESCUE A SURVIVOR FROM THE U.S.S. *WEST VIRGINIA* AFTER THE ATTACK ON PEARL HARBOR

Attack on Pearl Harbor

ACROSS

2. Japanese Admiral Yamamoto is quoted as saying all the Pearl Harbor attack did was to "___ a sleeping giant."

5. A ___ to the warship that sank in the harbor commemorates those lives lost.

7. Important facilities including oil ___ depots were not damaged in the attack.

8. In addition to aircraft, the Japanese used ___ in their attack on Hawaii.

13. The attack on Pearl Harbor was the first attack on a U.S. ___.

14. The empire of Japan felt the U.S. ___ was a threat to their domination of the Pacific.

15. President Roosevelt said before Congress that the attack on Pearl Harbor was a date that "will live in ___."

DOWN

1. A total of eight ___ were destroyed in the aerial attack on Pearl Harbor.

3. The U.S.S. ___ was struck four times and capsized in Pearl Harbor.

4. Bombs and ___ were dropped on the fleet in Pearl Harbor.

6. The U.S.S. ___ was a navy coastal minesweeper that was the first craft to detect a Japanese midget sub on the day of the attack.

9. Japanese fighter planes and ___ were involved in the attack on Pearl Harbor.

10. Three days after the U.S. declared war on Japan and the Axis powers, ___ and Italy declared war on the United States.

11. The Japanese attacked on a ___ morning, thinking the U.S. military would be less ready to respond.

12. Over 1,100 U.S. military personnel lost their lives on the U.S.S. ___, which sank in Pearl Harbor.

Breaking the Japanese Naval Code

The Japanese Naval Code, known as JN-25, was used to send military messages to generals during World War II. After the attack on Pearl Harbor, the goal of U.S. intelligence was to break the JN-25 code. The code consisted of groups of five-digit numbers. The code was encrypted by using an extra group of numbers, called an additive group. This additive group would be added or subtracted from the five-digit numbers to come up with a coded message. The code was successfully broken in time to forewarn of Japan's planned attack on Midway Island.

Try to decipher the number groups below by coming up with the letter that completes a word to fill in the sentence blank. Take each five-digit number and the additive group indicated above the number, and add the two numbers together. (When the total is two digits, drop the first digit and put the second digit on the total line.) Do not carry the first digit over to the next column. Then add up the digits from the total line and make that equal a letter of the alphabet from the chart below.

JAPANESE CODE   IMAGE BY ODACIR BLANCO

ADDITIVE GROUP 1	1	3	5	6	7	EXAMPLE					3	8	6	2	0
GROUP 2	4	5	3	1	8	ADDITIVE GROUP 3	2	7	6	9	1				
GROUP 3	2	7	6	9	1						5	5	2	1	1 = 14 = (total of five digits = N)
GROUP 4	9	5	0	7	4	Where there's a two-digit total, as in the second column, drop the first digit.
GROUP 5	3	2	7	2	6	The five-digit total equals the letter of the alphabet.

A	B	C	D	E	F	G	H	I	J	K	L	M	N	O	P	Q	R	S	T	U	V	W	X	Y	Z
1	2	3	4	5	6	7	8	9	10	11	12	13	14	15	16	17	18	19	20	21	22	23	24	25	26
27	28	29	30	31	32	33	34	35	36	37	38	39	40	41	42	43	44	45							

ADDITIVE GROUP 1	ADDITIVE GROUP 2	ADDITIVE GROUP 3	ADDITIVE GROUP 4	ADDITIVE GROUP 5
6 1 6 6 8	2 7 9 2 2	4 6 5 3 3	2 6 5 4 2	2 2 3 9 5
8 3 0 4 4	3 4 2 6 9	2 5 7 5 1	7 5 6 1 3	4 5 6 3 9
6 4 4 3 1	6 5 8 2 2	5 3 6 7 4	2 6 1 4 9	8 3 4 4 4
0 8 6 5 3	8 3 7 4 0	7 6 4 3 4	2 5 0 3 6	5 9 1 7 3
5 6 7 1 6	5 8 6 4 3	6 8 2 4 5	4 8 6 4 2	6 6 8 4 3
4 8 3 6 2	9 9 5 7 4	8 4 4 1 9	5 4 5 7 1	7 8 4 8 4
		6 8 3 0 7	7 3 8 2 2	5 0 8 5 8
			3 6 2 6 7	0 8 5 8 4

1. Pearl Harbor was attacked on a ___, as the Japanese felt that was when American military would least expect an attack.

2. The Battle of ___ turned the tide of war in the Pacific to the benefit of the Allies.

3. The ___ Declaration stated the terms of surrender for Japan.

4. The atomic bomb ending the war was dropped on ___.

5. Japanese suicide bombers launched ___ attacks on Allied ships and aircraft carriers.

Sudoku

ZERO

	R		
O		Z	
	O	E	
E			R

A JAPANESE ZERO FIGHTER PLANE   PHOTO BY MARC GROSSMAN

GUAM

U	M		A
	G		
		M	G

INFAMY

	Y	A		M	
N		I			
	F	M			I
			M		
	Y	N			F
	A		I		

MIDWAY

W					D
	I		Y	M	
				Y	A
	Y			I	
Y	A	M			
		M			Y

GUNBOATS

O		G		S			
			U	A			T
G	S			B		N	
		N			G		S
B		A					U
	G		S		B		
S	O				B		
			N		T	S	

SUBMARINE

B		U	S		R		M
M				I		N	
	S		M	A		B	
R		B		N	S		E
	E					U	
S		N		U			B
U		S	N		E		
E			R			M	
	B	M		I		S	A

AERIAL PHOTOGRAPH OF MIDWAY ATOLL

Battle of Midway

ACROSS
3. The Japanese were caught off guard by the American attack because they lacked ___.

5. The Japanese carrier *Soryu* was sunk as well as the carrier U.S.S. ___.

8. Bombers from the U.S.S. ___ attacked two Japanese aircraft carriers on June 4, 1942.

10. The Japanese aircraft carriers operating around Midway Island were commanded by Admiral ___.

11. American ___ breakers had intercepted Japanese communications, allowing the U.S. to prepare for Midway.

12. American Admiral Chester ___ led the U.S. operation against Japan at Midway.

14. The carrier that was used to launch the raid of Japan and at Midway was the U.S.S. ___.

15. After the battle, Midway Island was used as a ___ base for the remainder of the war.

DOWN
1. Thirty-seven Douglas ___ bombers conducted the attack on Japanese carriers at Midway.

2. The ___ Raid of Japan and Tokyo prompted the Japanese to plan an attack at Midway Island.

4. The Midway ___ is a ring-shaped island formed of coral.

6. The U.S. Navy defeated the ___ Japanese Navy in the Battle of Midway.

7. U.S. carrier forces at Midway were led by Rear Admiral Raymond A. ___.

9. Admiral Isoroku ___ planned a showdown with American forces at Midway.

11. A total of four Japanese aircraft ___ were destroyed at the Battle of Midway.

13. Of forty-one Japanese ___ bombers in the battle, thirty-five were shot down by U.S. attack craft.

Battle of Guadalcanal

A U.S. 11TH MARINES 75MM PACK HOWITZER AND CREW ON GUADALCANAL, SEPTEMBER OR OCTOBER 1942. U.S. NATIONAL ARCHIVES.

ACROSS

1. The Battle of Guadalcanal was given the code name Operation ___.

3. The first major battle of Guadalcanal involved U.S. Marines and the ___ Detachment of Japanese.

6. Possession of Guadalcanal was important for sea communication between the United States and ___.

7. The Battle of Guadalcanal was the first ___ campaign by U.S. ground forces.

8. A muddy airstrip captured by the marines on Guadalcanal was renamed ___ Field for the major killed in the Battle of Midway.

10. In an effort to take back the airfield, 6,000 Japanese troops invaded at night in the Battle of ___'s Ridge.

13. ___ Sound was the name given the stretch of water between Guadalcanal and the Florida Islands because of the number of sunken vessels there.

DOWN

2. The Allied code name for Guadalcanal Island was ___.

4. Both American and Japanese forces were weakened by ___ in insect-infested jungles.

5. The island of Guadalcanal was occupied by the ___ when the U.S. attacked in August 1942.

6. On August 7, 1942, the U.S. 1st Marine Division performed an ___ landing at Guadalcanal.

9. At the end of the battle the remaining defeated Japanese were evacuated from Cape ___.

11. The Japanese were headquartered in the northern end of the island chain at ___.

12. Guadalcanal is located in the ___ Island chain, in the southwest Pacific Ocean.

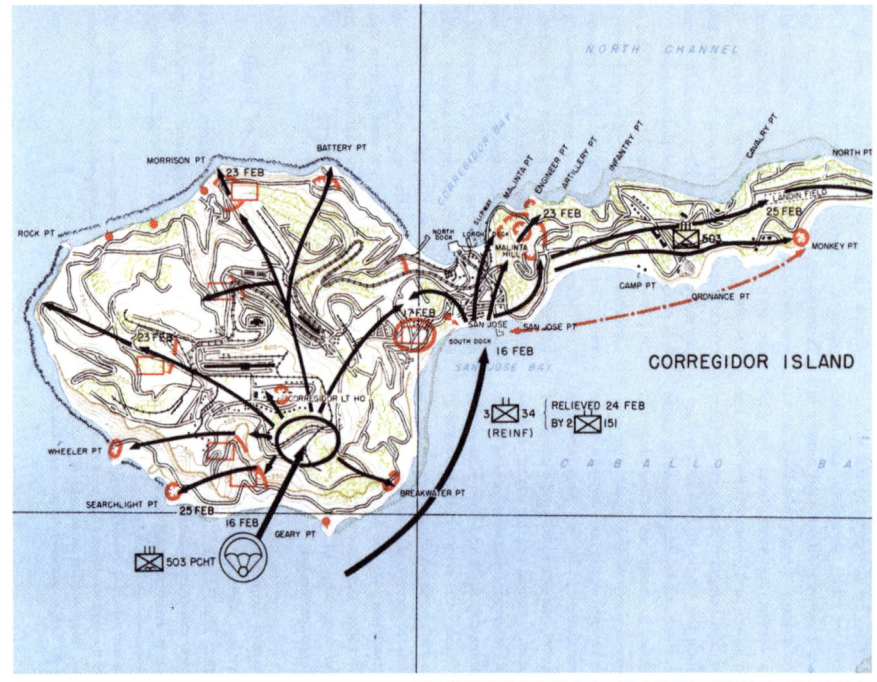

MAP SHOWING THE RECAPTURE OF CORREGIDOR ISLAND IN 1945

War in the Philippines

ACROSS
4. The ___, consisting of the islands of Guam and Tinian, were valued by the Allies because they were close to Japanese islands.

7. Philippine President Manuel ___ and Vice President Sergio Osmena went to the United States and set up a government in exile after the Japanese takeover of the islands.

8. The "Tiger of Malaya," Tomoyuki ___, was the army general who won the Battles of Malaya and Singapore for Japan.

10. The Battle of ___ was a monthlong bloodbath that ended three years of Japanese occupation in February-March 1945.

12. In April 1942, combined American-Filipino forces were defeated by the Japanese at the Battle of ___.

13. While the U.S. was victorious in the Battle of ___, it was the costliest in that nearly 3,000 Americans were killed.

DOWN
1. After losing the battle, over 60,000 American and Filipino troops were forced into the torturous ___ Death March.

2. Japan felt that taking the Philippines was important because of its strategic location and its being ___-rich.

3. General Douglas ___ was recalled from retirement to lead U.S. Army forces in the Far East and to mobilize the Philippine Army.

4. The second largest island of the Philippines, ___, was secured by Filipino guerillas and American troops in March 1945.

5. Just five days after the attack on Pearl Harbor, Japan invaded the island of ___ with ground troops.

6. The Japanese ___ had taken control of most of the Philippine islands by 1942.

9. Throughout WWII Filipino ___ forces fought the Japanese occupying their country.

11. The amphibious landing at the Battle of ___ Gulf was the first American-Filipino effort to retake the Philippines.

12. Japan's surprise attack on ___ Air Force Base on Pampanga took place December 8, 1941.

FIRST FLAG SET ATOP MOUNT SURIBACHI
PHOTO BY LOUIS R. LOWERY   LIBRARY OF CONGRESS

Battle of Iwo Jima

ACROSS

2. The February 19, 1945, landing of marines on Iwo Jima was known as Operation ___.

5. Marines raised the Stars and Stripes on the top of Mount ___, an extinct volcano.

6. Sea-to-land vehicles called ___ were used to land on the beach, but they sank in the volcanic sand of Iwo Jima.

10. When the Japanese mixed the island's volcanic ash with concrete, it created thick-walled reinforcements called ___.

12. A key weapon against the bunkers Japanese built on Iwo Jima were M4A3R3 ___ tanks, which were difficult to destroy.

13. B-24 ___ pounded Iwo Jima for seventy-four straight days before the invasion began.

DOWN

1. Iwo Jima was the one conflict in which the number of ___ on the winning side (the Americans) outnumbered that of the losers.

3. The Iwo Jima memorial is located at the entrance to ___ National Cemetery in Virginia.

4. Japanese Emperor Hirohito hand-picked Lieutenant General Tadamichi ___ to lead Japan's forces on Iwo Jima.

5. "Iwo Jima" means ___.

7. Major General Harry ___ V was commander of the U.S. operation on Iwo Jima.

8. In the final stages of fighting, air support came from P-51 ___.

9. The famous flag-raising was reenacted so that photographer Joe ___ could capture the moment of victory for the U.S.

11. U.S. Marines used explosives and flame___ to attack Japanese tunnels on the island.

GENERAL MACARTHUR WADES ASHORE AT LEYTE ISLAND   NARA

General Douglas MacArthur

ACROSS

4. General MacArthur oversaw Operation ___, designed to halt the Japanese at Rabaul, Papua New Guinea.

5. Douglas and his son Arthur were the first father and son both to be awarded the Medal of ___.

6. The Central ___ was formed from Australian intelligence and American code breakers to intercept and analyze Japanese signals.

7. After headquarters in Corregidor were bombed by the Japanese, MacArthur moved his base of operations to ___ .

10. The purpose of MacArthur's return to the Philippines in October 1944 was to lead aircraft carrier forces in the Battle of ___ Gulf.

12. In December 1944 MacArthur was awarded the rank of ___-___ general of the U.S. Army.

14. President ___ recalled Douglas MacArthur to active duty in the U.S. Army in July 1941.

15. General MacArthur led Allied forces to victory in the Battles of Luzon and ___ in the Philippines in January 1945.

DOWN

1. MacArthur was given the nickname "___" Doug by the troops remaining after Japanese attacks on Corregidor.

2. In 1915 Douglas MacArthur worked for the U.S. ___ Department.

3. On December 20, 1941, Douglas MacArthur was promoted to ___.

4. April 18, 1942, MacArthur was named supreme ___ of Allied forces in the southwest Pacific area.

8. By February 1942, with the Philippines under Japan's tight control, the president ordered General MacArthur to relocate to ___.

9. After the Japanese victory in the Philippines, MacArthur was quoted as saying, "I came through and I shall ___."

11. General MacArthur signed the Japanese surrender document aboard the U.S.S. ___.

13. Chief of Staff for the U.S. Army George ___ insisted that an Australian lead the Allied land forces, as most of the troops were Australian.

ADMIRAL CHESTER W. NIMITZ STEPS OUT OF A BUNKER ON MIDWAY ATOLL

Admiral Chester Nimitz

ACROSS

3. Chester Nimitz graduated from the U.S. Naval ___ in 1905.

5. Admiral Nimitz's first strategic victory in May 1942 involved carrier-to-carrier combat in the Battle of the ___ Sea.

7. The two-day Battle of the ___ Sea, which Nimitz oversaw, crippled Japan from being able to launch major aircraft carrier operations.

9. In June 1942, Nimitz led a victory that severely damaged the Japanese fleet in the Battle of ___.

11. December 14, 1944, Chester Nimitz was appointed ___ admiral by President Roosevelt.

13. Admiral Nimitz signed the Japanese instrument of ___ aboard the U.S.S. *Missouri* in Tokyo Bay.

14. Admiral ___ was given command of the Pacific Fleet in January 1941 after Nimitz turned it down in favor of more-senior officers getting the chance.

DOWN

1. Four months after the Pearl Harbor attack, March 24, 1942, Nimitz was named ___-in-chief of the U.S. Pacific Fleet.

2. One of Admiral Nimitz's chief duties as commander of the Pacific Fleet was to keep supply lines open between the U.S. and the ___ Islands.

4. President Truman presented Nimitz with a gold star for his third ___ Service Medal.

6. Admiral Nimitz's successful amphibious assaults were directed on Iwo Jima and ___.

8. In the period October 24–26, 1944, Nimitz's ships turned back powerful Japanese fleets in the Battle of ___ Gulf in the Philippines.

10. Admiral Nimitz was nominated chief of naval ___ following the war's end.

12. Nimitz moved the headquarters of the Pacific Fleet from Pearl Harbor to ___ in January 1945 until the war's end.

U.S.S. *INDIANA* BOMBARDS KAMAISHI, JULY 14, 1945

Pacific War Fast Facts

ACROSS

3. The ring of Japanese spies watching the U.S. Atlantic Fleet was based not in the United States, but in ___.

6. The Manhattan ___, charged with building an atomic bomb, was authorized by President Roosevelt.

9. The Japanese never cracked the code used by U.S. Marines, which was based on the ___ Indian language.

10. The only use of chemical weapons during the war was by Italy in Ethiopia and by Japan in ___.

11. In 1974, a Japanese soldier came out of hiding after twenty-nine years on the Pacific island of ___, unaware that his country had surrendered long before.

13. The name given the atomic bomb dropped on Hiroshima was ___ ___.

14. In Japan, an atomic bomb survivor is called *niju hibakusha*, which translates to "explosion-___ person."

DOWN

1. If a third atomic bomb had been necessary, ___ would have been the target.

2. Japan lost 4 aircraft carriers and 248 aircraft in the Battle of ___.

4. The Japanese launched over 9,000 small balloons with bombs in them that floated across the Pacific Ocean and killed six people in the state of ___.

5. ___ forced 120,000 Japanese-Americans from their homes in the U.S. after the Pearl Harbor bombing.

7. The term kamikaze, referring to Japanese fighter pilots dive-bombing Allied ships, translates in English to "___ wind."

8. The "___ of Bataan and Corregidor" were seventy-seven army and navy nurses who survived three years of Japanese captivity and continued caring for the injured after being liberated.

12. Twenty-three sets of ___ died on the U.S.S. *Arizona* in the attack on Pearl Harbor.

AFTERMATH OF ATOMIC BOMB EXPLOSION IN NAGASAKI   NARA

The Pacific War's End

ACROSS

3. The leaders of Japan were tried in the Tokyo War Crimes ___ in April 1946.

6. The Japanese carrier force was virtually destroyed in May 1944 after losing the Battle of ___.

7. The terms upon which the Japanese armed forces were to surrender were spelled out in the ___ Declaration.

8. Some argued that the U.S. naval ___ of Japan would have ended the war without the need for nuclear attacks.

11. More than a quarter of Japanese aircraft carriers and more than half of their merchant ships were destroyed by Allied ___.

13. General Curtis LeMay led the U.S. Army Air Force in Operation ___, in which Japanese waterways were mined by Allied aircraft.

15. Following Japan's surrender, its ___ was led by the supreme commander of the Allied powers, General Douglas MacArthur.

DOWN

1. The B-29 Superfortress that dropped the atomic bomb on Hiroshima was named the ___ Gay.

2. Operation ___, which was the Allied occupation of Japan, came to an end in September 1951.

4. The ___ of surrender by Japan was signed on September 2, 1945, in Tokyo Bay.

5. The second and last nuclear attack occurred three days after the first, at ___, Japan.

9. With few experienced pilots left, the Japanese turned to ___ attacks of Allied forces to cause the greatest casualties.

10. The first nuclear attack in history occurred when the Japanese city of ___ was bombed on August 6, 1945.

12. The surrender terms for Japan were written by Great Britain's Winston Churchill, Chairman Chiang Kai-shek of China, and President Harry ___ of the United States.

14. As Allied forces sought island bases closer to Japan, the Battle of ___ resulted in the death of 94 percent of the Japanese soldiers involved.

Names & Places of WWII

O	T	O	M	A	M	A	Y	E	C	H	A	M	A	R	P
A	J	I	N	E	T	E	N	T	O	N	H	R	E	O	E
N	E	V	I	G	E	O	K	I	N	A	W	A	T	U	A
G	U	K	A	P	L	U	H	A	S	N	S	B	Y	C	R
U	L	S	T	A	S	H	T	M	A	E	A	A	E	I	L
A	O	N	G	T	A	M	I	J	O	W	I	A	L	G	H
D	M	A	R	E	M	S	L	H	O	R	A	M	T	H	A
A	Y	A	B	O	R	I	T	A	C	S	N	A	E	A	R
L	F	O	M	A	S	N	D	R	H	I	O	C	S	A	B
C	N	R	C	Y	E	H	O	W	E	A	Z	A	T	D	O
A	N	E	H	R	A	W	R	D	A	H	I	R	A	W	R
N	I	M	I	T	Z	A	B	E	K	Y	R	T	N	I	T
A	R	O	D	I	G	E	R	R	O	C	A	H	L	N	E
L	P	H	I	L	I	P	P	I	N	E	S	U	B	K	L
R	E	A	M	I	H	S	O	R	I	H	S	R	A	Y	I
B	H	A	N	A	D	L	O	T	E	R	U	W	O	H	N

Pacific War Battles & Motherland

1 = e
2 = d
3 = b
4 = g
5 = f
6 = h
7 = i
8 = c
9 = a

Attack on Pearl Harbor

Breaking the Japanese Naval Code

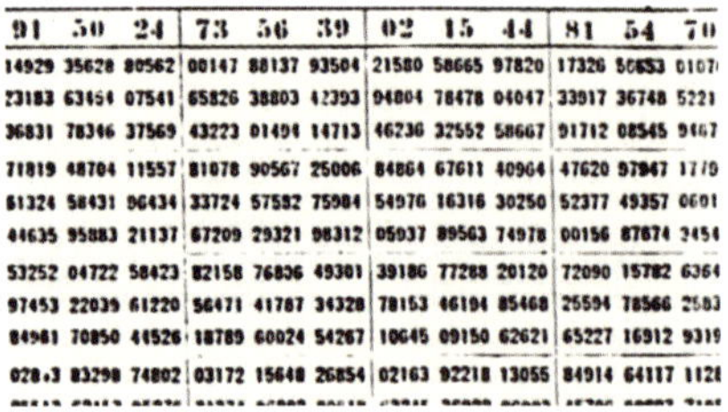

91	50	24	73	56	39	02	15	44	81	54	70
14929	35628	80562	00147	88137	93504	21580	58665	97820	17326	50653	0107
23183	63454	07541	65826	38803	42393	94804	78478	04047	33917	36748	5221
36831	78346	37569	43223	01494	14713	46236	32552	58667	91712	08545	9467
71819	48704	11557	81078	90567	25006	84864	67611	40964	47620	97947	1779
61324	58431	96434	33724	57582	75984	54976	16316	30250	52377	49357	0601
44635	95883	21137	67209	29321	98312	05937	89563	74978	00156	87874	2454
53252	04722	58423	82158	76836	49301	39186	77288	20120	72090	15782	6364
97453	22039	61220	56471	41787	34328	78153	46194	85468	25594	78566	2503
84981	70850	44526	18789	60024	54267	10645	09150	62621	65227	16912	9319
028+3	83298	74802	03172	15648	26854	02163	92218	13055	84914	64117	1128

SUNDAY
MIDWAY
POTSDAM
NAGASAKI
KAMIKAZE

Sudoku

ZERO

Z	E	R	O
O	R	Z	E
R	O	E	Z
E	Z	O	R

GUAM

U	M	G	A
G	A	U	M
M	G	A	U
A	U	M	G

INFAMY

F	I	Y	A	N	M
N	M	A	I	F	Y
A	F	M	N	Y	I
Y	N	I	F	M	A
I	Y	N	M	A	F
M	A	F	Y	I	N

MIDWAY

W	M	Y	I	A	D
D	I	A	Y	M	W
M	D	I	W	Y	A
A	Y	W	D	I	M
Y	A	D	M	W	I
I	W	M	A	D	Y

GUNBOATS

O	T	G	A	S	N	U	B
N	B	S	U	A	O	G	T
G	S	O	T	B	U	N	A
A	U	N	B	T	G	O	S
B	N	A	O	G	S	T	U
T	G	U	S	N	B	A	O
S	O	T	G	U	A	B	N
U	A	B	N	O	T	S	G

SUBMARINE

B	N	U	S	E	R	A	I	M
M	A	E	U	B	I	S	N	R
I	S	R	M	A	N	B	E	U
R	U	B	I	N	S	M	A	E
A	E	I	B	R	M	N	U	S
S	M	N	A	U	E	I	R	B
U	R	S	N	M	A	E	B	I
E	I	A	R	S	B	U	M	N
N	B	M	E	I	U	R	S	A

Battle of Midway

Battle of Guadalcanal

War in the Philippines

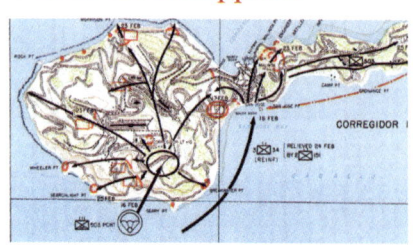

Battle of Iwo Jima

General Douglas MacArthur

Admiral Chester Nimitz

The Pacific War's End

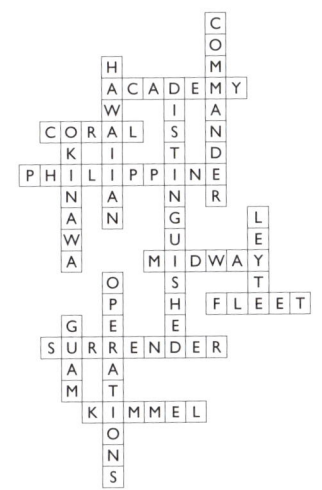

Pacific War Fast Facts

TOPICS
GRAB A PENCIL PRESS

Abraham Lincoln	John Fitzgerald Kennedy
American Flag	Natural History
American Revolution	New York City
Architecture	Presidents of the United States
Art History	Texas History
Benjamin Franklin	Washington, D.C.
Civil War History	World War II
Ellis Island and the Statue of Liberty	World War II European Theater
First Ladies	World War II Pacific Theater
George Washington	Yellowstone National Park

COMING SOON
Flight Puzzle Book
Korean War Puzzle Book
Library of Congress Puzzle Book
National Parks Puzzle Book
Secret Writing: A Code Breaker's Puzzle Book
Vietnam War Puzzle Book

GRAB A PENCIL PRESS

an imprint of Applewood Books
Carlisle, Massachusetts 01741
www.grabapencilpress.com

To order, call: 800-277-5312